OVER MIAMI

OVER MIAMI

AERIAL PHOTOGRAPHS AND TEXT BY **DAVID KING GLEASON**

LOUISIANA STATE UNIVERSITY PRESS

BATON ROUGE AND LONDON

Copyright © 1990 by Louisiana State University Press
All rights reserved
Manufactured in Japan
First printing
99 98 97 96 95 94 93 92 91 90   5 4 3 2 1

Designer: Laura Roubique Gleason
Typeface: Primer
Typesetter: G & S Typesetters, Inc.
Printer and binder: Dai Nippon Printing Co., Ltd.

Library of Congress Cataloging-in-Publication Data

Gleason, David K.
    Over Miami : aerial photographs and text / by David King Gleason.
        p.   cm.
    ISBN 0-8071-1635-1 (alk. paper)
    1. Miami (Fla.)—Aerial photographs.   2. Miami Region (Fla.)—
Aerial photographs.   3. Miami (Fla.)—Description—Views.   4. Miami
Region (Fla.)—Description and travel—Views.   I. Title.
    F319.M6G57   1990
    917.59′381′00222—dc20   90-5859
                                                             CIP

The paper in this book meets the guidelines for
permanence and durability of the Committee on
Production Guidelines for Book Longevity of the Council
on Library Resources.⊗

To my grandchildren: Rebecca and Andrew; Chrissie, Abbie, and Clair

Many thanks to the very capable pilots who
helped me complete this project: helicopter pilots
Paul Barth, Jean-Paul Robinson, Jean Pujol, Don
Bomback, Jr., and Bill Riggs; and fixed-wing fliers
Fred Cabanas and George Camollo. Beth Dunlop,
Jack Luft, and Mitch Kaplan always took time out
to check my progress and answer my myriad
questions.

    The capable staff at Gleason Photography man-
aged to run interference for me and keep the studio on an even keel during my preoccupation with
this book. Thanks again to Gisela O'Brien, who
made all the reproduction-grade prints; Craig
Saucier, in-house archivist; Peggy Galmon, our
housekeeper; Paige Dugas, receptionist; Cyndy
Branton, all-round utility person and favorite
daughter; and of course, my long-suffering and
everlovin' wife Josie, without whose love and sup-
port I simply wouldn't function.

CONTENTS

Foreword by Beth Dunlop   vii

PART ONE : The Miami River, Coconut Grove, and Coral Gables   1
PART TWO : Homestead to Opa-locka to Downtown   41
PART THREE : Key Biscayne, Biscayne Bay, and Miami Beach   69
PART FOUR : Broward and Palm Beach Counties   97
PART FIVE : Festive Miami   127

Index   135

IN MIAMI

1. Orange Bowl
2. The Atlantis
3. Vizcaya
4. Biscayne Bay Yacht Club
5. Miami City Hall
6. Barnacle
7. SW 8th Street—Calle Ocho—Tamiami Trail
8. Coral Gables City Hall
9. Biltmore Hotel
10. University of Miami
11. Charles Deering Estate
12. Metrozoo
13. Miami International Airport
14. Opa-locka City Hall
15. Hialeah Park
16. Joe Robbie Stadium
17. Calder Race Course
18. Monastery of Saint Bernard de Clairvaux
19. Florida International University
20. Barry University
21. Freedom Tower
22. Miami-Dade Community College
23. Bayfront Park

IN KEY BISCAYNE

24. Cape Florida Lighthouse
25. Key Colony Condominium

IN MIAMI BEACH

26. South Pointe
27. Fountainebleau
28. Flagler Island
29. Haulover Cut

BROWARD COUNTY

30. Pier 66
31. Hillsboro Lighthouse

PALM BEACH COUNTY

32. The Breakers

IN THE KEYS

33. John Pennecamp Coral Reef State Park
34. Alligator Reef Lighthouse

KEY WEST

35. Mallory Square
36. Fort Jefferson
37. Loggerhead Key

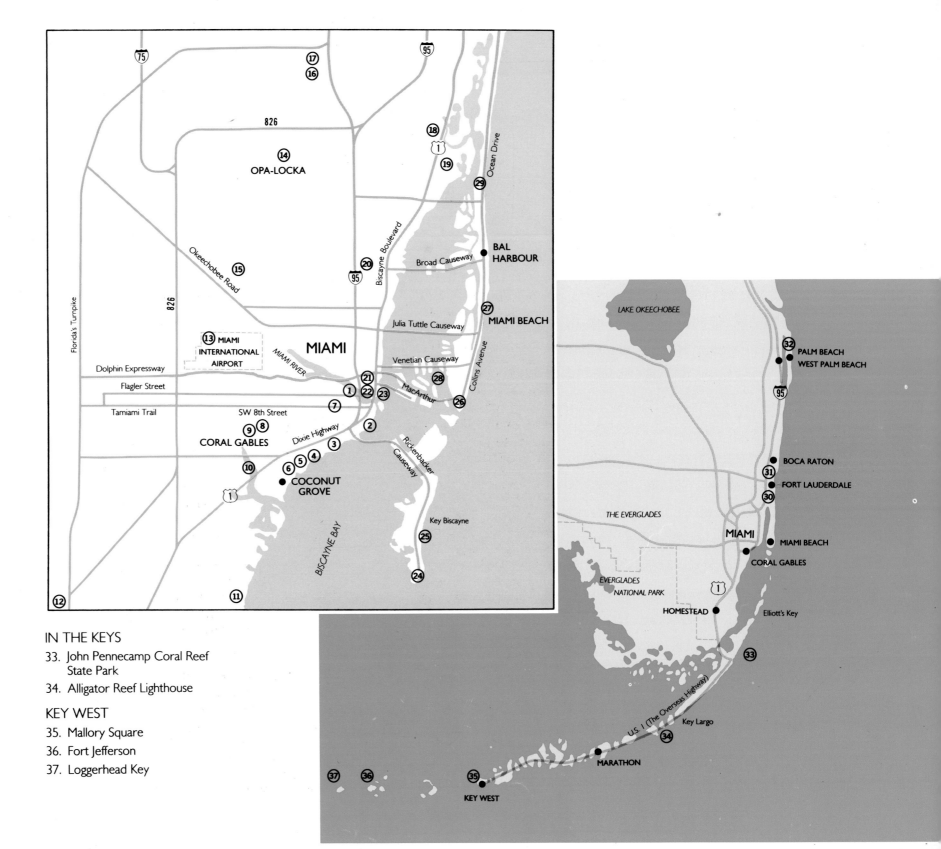

MAP BY CHET BO

FOREWORD

BETH DUNLOP
MIAMI *HERALD* ARCHITECTURE CRITIC

Miami is a city not merely of this century or of this decade, but of the moment. It gleams in the sunlight, and sometimes it seems so bright that it might just be a vast stage set, under the most theatrical of spotlights. We know that it is real, though, because it is at once vibrant and full of flaws, and because it is ever changing. In America, we are fascinated by newness, much as Italians are by antiquity; we show off our gleaming steel and stone office buildings as if they were our temples. Miami provides us with a half-finished metaphor for today, or tomorrow. There is myth as much as reality here. Part of that is its newness, but even in its short history, there has always been a temptation to make Miami into a mythological place.

Its low-lying land and endless blue skies provide the perfect tableau for fictitious towns with borrowed histories and invented architecture. Indeed, south Florida is so flat that we somehow seldom think of it as having a story or topography other than a man-made one. The land rises and falls little as it cuts a swath between ocean and swampland. Geography provides the foreground and the background: To the east is the Atlantic, to the west, the Everglades. And in between is paradise lost and found and maybe lost again—transformed into instant cities, rows of concrete block and stucco that did not seem to be there yesterday. In a world where other cities evolve over whole epochs, here is a place that has emerged, dense and populous, in little more than a century, a startling feat.

David King Gleason soared high and hovered low over this stretch of coastline, in helicopters and small planes, to tell this quite remarkable story. In his photographs, we get a sense of Miami's compressed and colorful history, of its dashing architecture, of its special relationship of land to water. From above Miami—above the stretch of south Florida from Key West to Palm Beach, land, barrier islands, keys, and all—a different, dramatic, complex landscape emerges.

Gleason's camera gives us much more of Miami than the expected postcard imagery of downtown or the beach; the aerial perspective takes us beyond the familiar views to a deeper understanding of a city and its region. And indeed, there is a complexity here, manifested in the sophistication of the downtown skyline, the glitter of Brickell, the swagger of hotels along Collins Avenue. Yet in the magnificent townscapes of Coral Gables and Palm Beach, there is still an intimacy. From on high, it is possible to see just how swiftly south Florida has developed, and that is perhaps the greatest genius of David Gleason's photographs—to give us a sense of the immediacy of it all. It is an impressive sight.

He has, appropriately, defined Miami in its largest sense, as the focus of a linear region stretching some 200-plus miles along the Atlantic from Palm Beach to Key West. Miami is indeed the metropolis, with all that implies: danger, grandeur, sophistication, confusion. And yet, rightly so, Gleason, seeing it from on high, knows how to put Miami in its place. He has given it a geographic context and a social milieu—from Christmas boat parades in Fort Lauderdale, a flotilla of decorated yachts, to street festivals in Little Havana, with crowds of cele-

brants—and even an economic setting: This is the region not just of tourism, cruise ships, and exports to South America but also of sugarcane plantations and winter tomato crops.

Before the 1870s, south Florida had little more than sporadic encampments. Key West, strategically placed at the tip of a string of little islands that curl out beyond the peninsula, was the southernmost city. Coconut Grove was just a settlement of a few seafarers; the brave handful—and it was literally a handful—who had landed in Fort Lauderdale were building houses close to the New River. Palm Beach, though it is hard to think of it in this context, was still mostly the coastal wilds. There was a single boardinghouse for winter visitors, called Cocoanut Grove House.

Henry Flagler, the railroader and hotelier, came to Palm Beach in 1893 and began building—hotels and his own last home, a mansion he called Whitehall. He intended Palm Beach to be his last stop, but in the frigid Florida winter of 1895 a tenacious transplant from Cleveland named Julia Tuttle persuaded him to continue his railroad to frost-free Miami. A year later Flagler's railroad arrived, and the city of Miami was born. That is for the record only, for we can little chart those early days; with the exception of a few houses and churches, the nineteenth-century buildings of south Florida are gone. Those that remain are relics—museums or monuments or oddities (the one extant Flagler workers house is now a restaurant)—and not a record of history.

A second, more lasting south Florida, sup-

planting the earlier one, was built just decades later, during the boomtime that culminated in the vast real estate crash of 1926. Before it did, whole cities were carved out of citrus groves—or mangroves and muck. We regard this as our primary architectural heritage in south Florida, and today, architects are casting back to this period for sources for new designs. Coral Gables has enacted a zoning ordinance that encourages the construction of new Mediterranean Revival buildings on a large scale, and the developers are following suit. Miami is constantly reinventing itself.

It was the construction of Vizcaya, more than any other building, that set the stage for the remarkable Mediterranean-style landscape of boomtime south Florida. The industrialist-heir James Deering erected a northern-Italian palace on the edge of Biscayne Bay. With its gardens and follies, Vizcaya showed that in south Florida it was possible to create a total landscape, a world within a world, imaginary and yet real. The impact of Vizcaya was extraordinary.

Much of what was to become boomtime south Florida followed on the heels of Vizcaya. Palm Beach came first, starting in 1918 when sewing-machine heir Paris Singer engaged the gentleman architect Addison Mizner to build the Everglades Club on Worth Avenue. Although it began as a hospital, the Everglades soon became the first of the town's exclusive new buildings and, perhaps just as important, established a captivating new architectural style that seemed to give Palm Beach the imprint of age, the aura of another world. The Everglades was followed

vii

quickly by the first of Mizner's many Palm Beach mansions, large and glamorous in a Spanish-Moorish-Venetian style that was his own invention.

Then came Coral Gables, an alluring new city with broad curving boulevards, plazas, fountains. Its architecture was an Italian-Spanish pastiche that we have come to know as Mediterranean Revival: thick stucco walls with elaborate stone trim, twisted Corinthian-capped columns, and lots of arches. The developer of Coral Gables, a minister's son named George Merrick, wanted to build "castles in Spain" where grapefruit used to grow; he wanted his city to be America's Riviera, and that is how he advertised it. The architects of Coral Gables—many of them protégés of Mizner—took storybook drawings rife with romance and translated them into equally romantic reality. The Biltmore Hotel, its tower a rendition of Seville's famous Giralda set into a Tuscan-palazzo base, was to be the centerpiece of Coral Gables; its architects, the New York firm of Schultze & Weaver, in a few short years left a heavy imprint on south Florida.

Coral Gables was the biggest and most visionary of the winter real estate boomtowns, but there were others, too, built rapidly and buoyed by optimism, ambition, and sunshine: Miami Shores, Hollywood, Fort Lauderdale, Boca Raton (Mizner's second Florida venture, this time as both architect and developer), Delray Beach, Boynton Beach, Lake Worth—towns big and small, the products of utopian dreamers and nefarious schemers. Some grew up over earlier settlements, and some started from scratch; but every development luxuriated in the picturesque possibilities of the place. Fort Lauderdale was crisscrossed with canals; those were not the days of attempting to protect the ecosystem. Carl Fisher created Miami Beach out of scrub.

For a time, this was south Florida's idyll, fulfilling a destiny as utopia at the end of the railroad. But starting with a killer hurricane on Labor Day weekend in 1926, the proverbial bubble burst. Developers went bankrupt, leaving half-finished towns, half-finished roads. The Great Depression came early to south Florida, and left early, as well. By the early 1930s, there was a new, if smaller, building boom under way, one that would result in a district only now becoming fully appreciated. That area is Miami Beach's delightful Art Deco district, a mile-square national historic district with more than eight hundred small stucco buildings constructed between World War I and World War II, most of them in the late 1930s. The architecture ranges from early Spanish and Mediterranean buildings to streamline moderne, the most austere of the Art Deco variations. But in the main these are pastel-painted capriccios, buildings with finials and spires, porthole windows and whimsical details, ranging from mermaids to Mayan motifs. The Art Deco district is a testimony to Miami's ability to triumph over adversity, for it emerged with all its good humor during some of the harshest years of America's history.

As World War II waned, south Florida found new life. Returning soldiers set out to make a new start for themselves, and in the next few decades, they did so in the fast-growing subdivisions of south Florida. As new development sprawled west—which it continues to do still at a rapid pace, in near defiance of a tricky ecology—the tourists too began to flock to south Florida. Morris Lapidus gave full-blown expression to the most lavish of fantasies, first at the Fontainebleau Hotel, which he filled with gilt and crystal and brocaded Baroque furniture. Next came the Eden Roc, another Lapidus concoction, and then followed a whole series of hotels that lined Collins Avenue, replacing beachfront mansions. But the reverie of Miami Beach in the fifties and sixties soon gave way to a more pragmatic rendition of paradise, and the oceanfront began to fill—from Miami Beach north to Palm Beach—with retirement condominiums, most of them dull concrete slabs that blocked the breezes and helped erode the beach. South Florida is more protective of its waterfront now, but much of it has been usurped.

The rise of Castro to power in Cuba brought a different kind of reality to Miami as thousands upon thousands of refugees flooded in. The old Miami *News* Tower, designed in 1925 by Schultze & Weaver as another version of the Giralda, became the processing center for these new arrivals and was renamed the Freedom Tower. Even today, dwarfed by newer and taller structures, the Freedom Tower holds its own, a beacon to ships arriving in the port, a true landmark. Miami became a bilingual and, more interestingly, bicultural city, and SW 8th Street—Calle Ocho—became the lively focal point of the area known as Little Havana. Ultimately, the immigrant population of Miami came from all across Central and South America and the Caribbean; today, Little Haiti provides a colorful counterpoint to Calle Ocho.

It was against this backdrop that modern Miami emerged, a cosmopolitan city with a sophisticated skyline that just ten years ago was gap-toothed. Miami has become the center of international trade for a hemisphere, and the buildings that now line Brickell Avenue, Miami's financial district, have the brittle shimmer of the money that made them possible. Downtown Miami has a strong silhouette dominated by just two towers: Southeast Financial Center, designed by E. Charles Bassett of Skidmore, Owings & Merrill; and CenTrust, designed by I. M. Pei & Partners. Each of these has a powerful presence: Southeast, because its pale granite changes so as the light shifts; CenTrust, the sleeker of the two, because of the dramatic way it is illuminated at night in colored lights.

The image of downtown Miami is really an imposed image, with buildings designed by outsiders defining it. Even the bayfront bears the imprint of others. Bayfront Park, long a neglected and tree-laden front yard to Miami, has been recast by the late sculptor Isamu Noguchi. Next to the park is Bayside, a coral-colored waterfront marketplace designed by the Cambridge, Massachusetts, architectural firm of Benjamin Thompson & Associates. Bayside has a tropical lilt to it, its buildings reflecting the architecture of the Caribbean, its coloration drawn from Vizcaya. In the end, in Miami or any other city, we see ourselves as others see us.

In the 1980s, two separate Miami-bred architectural movements began to change the image of south Florida. The first and most apparent of these was the work of Arquitectonica, the firm that designed the three flamboyant, brightly colored condominiums along the residential section of Brickell—the Palace, the Imperial, and the Atlantis—and other buildings, the North Dade Courthouse, Miracle Center. Arquitectonica uses bold colors and outsized geometry in designs that break down preconceptions, that surprise and charm. The inheritor in many ways of the stage-set tradition of Addison Mizner or Morris Lapidus, Arquitectonica moves it to a new level—abstraction. The second force shaping south Florida is far from iconoclastic; it springs from classical roots, from a desire to take the best of American design traditions and use them not just in the design of specific buildings but in the planning of whole towns and cities. The impact of this latter movement will be felt not so much in the downtown skyline or in the flashy forefront buildings as in urban neighborhoods and in suburbia.

The remarkable—and truly quite beautiful—collection of photographs to follow is more than a mere record of urban history. It shows south Florida at work and at play. There are no pictures of individuals here; people simply fill a stadium or sail a boat. But though these photographs were taken from distant points on high, there is an underlying humanity to them as well as a recognition that this is a special, and different, place. There are lots of landmarks to be seen here, lots of special places—famous houses, famous churches, famous islands—and it is a thrill to see them from this unique vantage point. These are not architectural photographs in which buildings become objects, but panoramas in which everything somehow fits together.

One amazement worth noting: David King Gleason's aerial photos are taken only in moving vehicles, and he prides himself on finding new vantage points. It is an effective tool for his own discipline, and it provides us with absorbing photographs as a source of both knowledge and fascination. And it is true that there are virtually no opportunities to see Miami this way save a glimpse of Brickell from the expressway, a moment sustained at fifty-five miles per hour, or a plane descent over Port Everglades or Palm Beach or the causeways that link Miami Beach to Miami. Those are fleeting moments; the joy of these photographs is that those ephemeral glimpses have been made permanent.

PART ONE

THE MIAMI RIVER, COCONUT GROVE, AND CORAL GABLES

◄

MIAMI, MID-1920s

In an early photograph by Miami Aerial Views, the young city's first skyscraper, the Miami *News* Tower (completed in 1925), dominates this view looking south along Biscayne Boulevard toward the Miami River.

Across old Biscayne Drive (now Biscayne Boulevard, paralleling the natural shoreline) were a rail terminal and the port of Miami. The creation of Bayside Park was well under way, with a marina visible at center left. The Royal Palm Hotel (demolished in 1930) and its extensive grounds were on the north bank of the Miami River.
Photo courtesy Historical Association of Southern Florida

▶

DOWNTOWN MIAMI, 1989

About the only building along Biscayne Boulevard recognizable from the 1920s is the Miami *News* Tower, La Giralda, restored in 1988 and now called the Freedom Tower. In the foreground is the site of the Gran Prix of Miami auto race held each February. South of the track are the Bayside Marketplace and Bayside Park.

◄

MIAMI AND THE VENETIAN CAUSEWAY, 1930s

Collins Bridge was the first span to link Ocean Beach, now Miami Beach, with the mainland. The wooden bridge across Biscayne Bay was built in 1913 at the instigation of John Collins. It was replaced in 1925 by the Venetian Causeway (then called the Venetian Way), in the foreground of this 1930s photograph. On the northern side of Biscayne Island was an airport; its hangar was at the western (right center) end of the island. Beyond Biscayne Island is Watson Island, still being filled in, and downtown Miami.

Photo courtesy Historical Association of Southern Florida

►

BISCAYNE ISLAND AND DOWNTOWN MIAMI, 1989

The airport on Biscayne Island gave way many years ago to waterfront homes and condominiums, but Watson Island still has a marina where steamships used to dock. It also serves as a helicopter and seaplane port. Two buildings visible in the 1930s aerial photograph are still standing: the Freedom Tower and the pyramid-topped Dade County Courthouse (1928)—each, when first built, the tallest on the skyline.

◄

CRUISE SHIPS AT DODGE ISLAND

Dodge Island, just south of Biscayne and Watson islands, is the home of the port of Miami, the busiest cruise ship port in the nation, serving nine cruise lines and 2.7 million passengers annually. Dodge and adjacent Lummus Island constitute the southernmost deepwater container port in the United States.

►

THE MIAMI RIVER AND DOWNTOWN

In this view (looking northeast across the Miami River and downtown Miami), the islands of Biscayne Bay and Miami Beach stretch across the background. The two tallest buildings are the 47-story CenTrust Tower, at left, designed by I. M. Pei & Partners, and the 55-story Southeast Financial Center, toward the right. On the north bank of the river, at lower left, are a small yellow building, the Flagler Workers House (1899), and the James L. Knight International Center, a concert hall and convention center connected to the Hyatt Regency Hotel just west of the Brickell Avenue bridge. Fort Dallas, a U.S. military outpost periodically occupied between the 1820s and 1850s, stood at right, where the river meets the bay.

◄
DAWN ON THE MIAMI RIVER

The newest span across the Miami River is the Metrorail bridge (foreground), adorned with a 3,600-foot-long neon "light sculpture" by Rockne Krebs. Beyond the Metrorail bridge are the Miami Avenue and Brickell Avenue bridges. To the east, in the background, are Dodge and Lummus islands, Miami Beach, and the Atlantic Ocean.

▶
FLAGLER WORKERS HOUSE

When Henry Morrison Flagler was building his Royal Palm Hotel (its grounds included the area where this house presently stands), he housed his supervisory employees in the Royal Palm Cottages—about thirty homes similar to this one. Overlooking the Miami River, the restored house, the only one remaining, is now a restaurant located in Fort Dallas Park.

JOSÉ MARTÍ PARK

On the south bank of the Miami River, just to the west of the I-95 bridge, is José Martí Park, named for the famous Cuban poet and patriot José Martí (1853–1895), who devoted his life to Cuban independence.

CARGO BOATS ON THE MIAMI RIVER

Farther to the west on the Miami River is a docking and loading area for small boats bound for Haiti and other Caribbean islands. Cargo for the return trip to the islands includes stoves, metal cabinets, refrigerators, plastic jugs, and hundreds of used bicycles.

◄

ORANGE BOWL STADIUM

The home field of the University of Miami Hurri-
canes, 1987 and 1989 national college football
champions, the Orange Bowl stadium, seating
more than 74,000, is the centerpiece of the
Orange Bowl Festival. Associated activities take
place annually from early November to late February, and include the Rolex/Orange Bowl International Tennis Championships, a regatta series for
professional and collegiate sailors, a 5-km run and
a 10-km race, a marathon, the King Orange Jamboree Parade held New Year's Eve, and the Federal Express/Orange Bowl Football Classic on New
Year's Day.

Downtown Miami is to the east, in the upper
left; condominiums along Brickell Avenue are toward the upper right.

▶

BRICKELL AVENUE: THE FINANCIAL
DISTRICT

When NE 2nd Avenue crosses the Miami River, it
becomes Brickell Avenue (running from bottom
center toward the top in this early morning view),
continuing south along Biscayne Bay to Coconut
Grove.

Near downtown, office buildings of financial
institutions form a glass and steel canyon along
Brickell Avenue. The district is said to contain the
largest concentration of international banking offices in the country.

◄

BRICKELL AVENUE CONDOMINIUMS

South of the financial district, architectural award–winning condominiums on Brickell Avenue overlook Biscayne Bay and Key Biscayne. The Palace, left, the Villa Regina, center, and the Imperial, right, were built in the late 1970s and early 1980s. The Villa Regina was designed by William Dorsky & Associates and was painted its many hues by Israeli artist Yacov Agam. The Palace and the Imperial were designed by the Coral Gables firm Arquitectonica International Corporation.

►

THE ATLANTIS

Arquitectonica also designed the striking 21-story Atlantis, completed in 1983. The designers placed a "skycourt" through the building between the twelfth and sixteenth floors and accented it with a 4-story palm tree and a Jacuzzi hot tub. With a different "high-tech" look to each facade, the Atlantis has been much in demand as a location for television and motion picture productions.

◀

VIZCAYA MUSEUM AND GARDENS

Vizcaya—"an elevated place"—is one of the great houses of America. Constructed in 1916 by James Deering, a co-heir of International Harvester Company, Vizcaya was built to give the impression of a great Italian villa, continuously occupied and evolving for more than 400 years.

Three architects were involved in the creation of the 38,000-square-foot house and its 15-acre estate: F. Burrall Hoffman, Jr., who designed the buildings; Diego Suarez, who planned the gardens; and Paul Chalfin, who was the general artistic supervisor. Vizcaya took two years to build and required a 1,000-man work force.

Deering wintered at Vizcaya until his death in 1925. In 1952 his heirs sold the estate to Dade County for a million dollars. Vizcaya, a self-sustaining museum of European decorative arts, is a division of the Metro-Dade Park and Recreation Department.

▶

VIZCAYA, THE EAST FACADE

The Villa Rezzonico, a seventeenth-century villa near Venice, was the inspiration for the east facade of Vizcaya. It overlooks Biscayne Bay and a great stone barge that acts as a breakwater, creating a small-craft harbor. Deering often came to Vizcaya by boat.

◄

ERMITA DE LA CARIDAD

A conical shrine to Our Lady of Charity faces the
bay south of Vizcaya. Ninety feet high and eighty
feet in diameter at ground level, the shrine inside
is oriented inside so that worshipers face toward
Cuba, whose history is illustrated in a mural above
the altar.

►

GROVE ISLE

Off Bayshore Drive up the shoreline from Coconut
Grove is a 26-acre artificially made island that
contains a hotel, apartments, and a private club.
Within the lobbies, the developer Martin C. Margulies displays examples from his personal art collection. Along the bayside walk are a number of
large works by well-known contemporary sculp-
tors, including Willem de Kooning, Isamu Noguchi, and Alexander Calder.

18

◄

SILVER BLUFF

Between downtown Miami and Coconut Grove, south along Biscayne Bay, is one of the last remnants of a bluff of oolitic limestone that once extended two miles down the bay and a half mile inland. The area of Silver Bluff began as a subdivision in 1911, was incorporated in 1921, and was annexed by the city of Miami in 1925. A historical marker (lower center) alongside Bayshore Drive describes the history and importance of the bluff.

►

BISCAYNE BAY AND CORAL REEF YACHT CLUBS

The second-oldest yacht club in the South, Biscayne Bay Yacht Club (center) was organized in 1887 and held its first regatta in February of that year. The present building, erected in 1932 on South Bayshore Drive, was designed by Walter De Garmo, who also had been the architect of an earlier, 1909 clubhouse. Club members have included Ernest Hemingway, Marshall Field, Andrew Carnegie, and Charles W. Armour.

To the right of the BBYC is the Coral Reef Yacht Club, whose clubhouse, a Venetian mansion built in about 1922 by Clifford Cole, was purchased by the club in 1955. The mansion had been owned in the 1950s by George Engle, then owner of the Coconut Grove Playhouse. At left center is Monty Trainer's Bayshore Restaurant.

MIAMI CITY HALL AND DINNER KEY MARINA

In 1931, on what was originally a small island used for picnicking by early residents of Coconut Grove, Pan American Airways built its "Air Gateway between the Americas," the world's largest seaplane terminal at that time and the country's most active commercial seaplane facility in the 1930s and early 1940s. During World War II, it became a U.S. Navy base. President Roosevelt boarded a seaplane there to fly to Casablanca.

Pan American sold the property to the city of Miami in 1946, and Dinner Key became a waterfront park. In 1954, Miami made the former terminal building its city hall.

THE BARNACLE

One of the early settlers of Coconut Grove was Commodore Ralph Middleton Munroe, a native of Concord, Massachusetts. Munroe, a yachtsman, photographer, and yacht designer, first visited Biscayne Bay in 1877. He was one of the founders of the Biscayne Bay Yacht Club.

In 1891, when Coconut Grove had 101 permanent residents, the commodore built the Barnacle facing the bay. At first only a single story high, but eight feet off the ground, the house was raised in 1908 to add a second, ground floor to meet the needs of Munroe's expanding family.

The Barnacle was owned by Munroes until the state of Florida bought it in 1973 and made it a state historic site.

23

COCONUT GROVE

Before Henry Flagler brought his Florida East Coast Railroad to the north bank of the Miami River in 1896, spawning the modern city of Miami, Coconut Grove was considered the largest community in south Florida.

Although it was annexed by Miami in 1925, the Grove still retains its identity, highlighted by some of the oldest residences in south Florida, Mediterranean villas, and tree-shaded streets that sometimes follow the paths of old pioneer trails.

In this view, Main Highway winds southward from the bottom of the picture, past the Coconut Grove Playhouse (1927), for thirty years a motion picture theater and a nationally known legitimate theater since 1956.

EL JARDIN

Built in 1917 upon ten exotically landscaped acres, John Bindley's Mediterranean Revival winter home enjoyed a pristine view of the bay in Coconut Grove at Main Highway (which runs across the top third of this photograph). Bindley was president of Pittsburgh Steel. The Spanish-tiled roof covers a 2½-story house with a central courtyard.

Now the Carrollton School for Girls operated by the Society of the Sacred Heart (another school building now lies between the house and the highway), the grounds of El Jardin (The Garden) are adjacent to land (right) once owned by William Jennings Bryan.

Bryan Memorial Church was built in 1926 fronting Main Highway. Across the highway can be seen the towers of the 1917 Plymouth Congregational Church.

25

◀

SW 8th STREET AND THE TAMIAMI TRAIL

A 1931 aerial view looks eastward over SW 8th Street. West Flagler and SW 1st Street intersect SW 22nd Avenue Road at lower left, and SW 8th Street, the Tamiami Trail (in the middle of the photograph), heads toward an unfettered view of Biscayne Bay. Government Cut is in the distance. The diagonally oriented streets of Brickell Hammock (center right) have few residences along them, but the then-new locality of Shenandoah (lower right) is moderately well developed.

Photo courtesy Historical Association of Southern Florida

▶

CALLE OCHO

Cuban refugees from Fidel Castro's regime thirty years ago tended to settle first in the older neighborhoods west of downtown Miami in the vicinity of SW 8th Street. The area, with its bilingual billboards and street signs, is now called Little Havana.

SW 8th Street is well known as Calle Ocho and is the locus for the Calle Ocho Festival in mid-March, which draws a million revelers for the weekend party celebrating the heritage of Cuba.

◄

PLAZA DE LA CUBANIDAD

On the southwest corner of Flagler Street and Teddy Roosevelt Avenue (SW 17th Avenue), a monument displays a large copper sculpture of the island of Cuba and a quotation from José Martí, a Cuban patriot in that island's struggle for independence from Spain: "Las Palmas son novias que esperan" (The palm trees are girlfriends who will wait).

►

BRIGADE 2506 MEMORIAL

An eternal flame burns at the monument dedicated to members of Brigade 2506 who died in the ill-fated Bay of Pigs invasion of Cuba in 1961. The memorial, at the corner of Calle Ocho and Memorial Boulevard (SW 13th Avenue), forms the north end of a block-long park celebrating Cuban history.

◀

DOUGLAS AND COUNTRY CLUB PRADO ENTRANCES

George Merrick, the founder of Coral Gables, envisioned his Mediterranean style development as an ancient European community, with monumental gates to the city. Merrick's uncle, artist and illustrator Denman Fink, architect Walter De Garmo, and Phineas Paist designed the million-dollar Douglas Entrance to Coral Gables, which opened in May of 1927. The complex included an arched gateway, tower, and associated galleries and shops on the northeast corner of Coral Gables at Douglas Road and 8th Street, the Tamiami Trail. The Douglas Entrance is listed on the National Register of Historic Places.

At Coral Gables' northwest corner, where the Tamiami Trail meets Country Club Prado, Merrick spent another million dollars on a block-long, formal Italian garden, the Prado Entrance, completed in 1927.

▶

VENETIAN POOL

A unique solution to the problem of what to do with a Coral Gables eyesore was solved in the mid-1920s by Denman Fink and Phineas Paist when they turned an old limestone quarry into a Venetian lagoon. Listed on the National Register of Historic Places, the Venetian Pool was used not only as a swimming pool (drained daily, not chlorinated, until 1986), but also, when drained, as an amphitheater.

At the converted quarry, operatic tenors sang and William Jennings Bryan spoke. Johnny Weismuller and Esther Williams, Olympic swimmers and motion picture stars, swam in the waters of the Venetian Pool.

MIRACLE CENTER AND THE MIRACLE MILE

Designed by Arquitectonica International Corporation, the Miracle Center (bottom right) is an exciting structure combining a shopping mall, theaters, and a health club on the lower floors, parking above, and a swimming pool and covered track on the top. Marbleized trapezoidal panels that float in front of the parking floors enliven the building's exterior.

Miracle Center faces SW 22nd Street where banyan trees, planted in the median in 1929, arch over the boulevard. The banyans end at Douglas Road (top third). Miami becomes Coral Gables, and 22nd Street becomes Coral Way, the first four blocks of which are known as the Miracle Mile, the leading shopping and commercial boulevard of Coral Gables.

COLONNADE BUILDING

For his sales offices, George Merrick created the monumental Colonnade Building on the Miracle Mile, using the services of Phineas Paist, Walter De Garmo, and Paul Chalfin, who was the general artistic supervisor for the construction of Vizcaya.

The Colonnade (foreground, along with shops on the Miracle Mile) is topped by a Spanish-tiled roof over a 75-foot-high rotunda. The building has served as a branch bank and, in World War II, as a navy pilot training center. Its rotunda has been a motion picture studio, as well as a basketball court for wartime student pilots. The Italianate landmark was renovated in 1985 by Intercap Investments and is now connected to an adjacent high-rise hotel and office building that echoes the roofline of the Colonnade rotunda.

32

33

◄
CORAL GABLES WATER TOWER

George Merrick's attention to detail carried all the
way to Coral Gables' two original water towers,
which he built in 1924 to resemble lighthouses.
One tower was destroyed by the 1926 hurricane
that severely damaged the area, but the other continued to function until 1931. It stands at the in-
tersection of Alhambra Circle, Greenway Court,
and Ferdinand Street.

►
CORAL GABLES CITY HALL

Built after the hurricane of 1926, which ended
the real estate boom in Coral Gables, the Coral
Gables City Hall was designed by Phineas Paist
and Denman Fink. It opened in February of 1928,
financed with bond issues totaling $200,000.

  The Spanish Mediterranean structure, built
with native Miami oolite (also called coral rock),
has an east-facing, semicircular columned wing
overlooking Miracle Mile. At the top of the building is a 3-tiered tower with a clock and 500-pound
bell.

THE BILTMORE HOTEL

Coral Gables' magnificent landmark hotel (built from 1925 to 1926) was designed by Schultze & Weaver, architects of the Waldorf-Astoria in New York, The Breakers hotel in Palm Beach, and the Miami *News* Tower, La Giralda. Its central 26-story tower is said to have been inspired by the Giralda bell tower of the cathedral of Seville in Spain.

Tile and marble used in the hotel came from Cuba and Italy. Place settings in the paneled, gold-ceilinged dining room were by Tiffany's, and diners were treated to pheasant and trout while they watched a revue of the latest New York and Paris fashions.

The complex included two golf courses, tennis courts, a polo field, bridle path, an area for fox hunting, and a swimming pool holding 1.25 million gallons of water.

During World War II, the Biltmore became a military hospital, and then served as a Veterans Administration hospital until 1968. Unoccupied for the next seventeen years, the Biltmore was renovated as a luxury hotel and office complex in 1985.

◄
CHINESE VILLAGE

Although George Merrick planned Coral Gables as a Mediterranean city, for diversity he located several "villages"—Italian, French Normandy, French City, French Country, Colonial, Italian, Dutch South African, and Chinese—within the city limits. More were planned but never completed because of the local economic crash, which followed the 1926 hurricane, and the Great Depression in 1929.

The Chinese Village (1926) has eight oriental-styled residences within a walled compound, near the Coral Gables waterway.

▶
DUTCH SOUTH AFRICAN VILLAGE

Palm Beach architect Marion Syms Wyeth designed the Dutch South African Village (1925) after the Baroque-style farmhouses of Dutch colonists in South Africa. Four homes are included in the village, located on a triangle formed by LeJeune Road, Riviera Drive, and Maya Street in Coral Gables.

◄
UNIVERSITY OF MIAMI

South of the Biltmore Hotel and Country Club is the 260-acre main campus of the University of Miami, chartered in 1925. George Merrick, founder of Coral Gables, donated 160 acres and $5 million to begin construction of the new campus.

The Norman Whitten University Center and the university bookstore flank the large swimming pool on Lake Osceola. Behind the student center at middle left is the Otto G. Richter Library, with science and engineering buildings behind it. At center right are the graduate school, the business school, and the Merrick building. In the middle ground at right is Doctor's Hospital.

PART TWO

HOMESTEAD TO OPA-LOCKA TO DOWNTOWN

◄
PARROT JUNGLE

Located south of Coral Gables, not far from Biscayne Bay at Red Road and SW 112th Street, Parrot Jungle is built on a natural south Florida hammock with a lake in the middle. One of Miami's oldest tourist attractions, Parrot Jungle is the residence of about seventy-five Caribbean flamingos and displays more than a thousand tropical birds. Alligators, tortoises, and iguanas, orchids, bougainvillaeas, and banana trees thrive in this Florida jungle setting, first opened in 1936.

►
CHARLES DEERING ESTATE

On Biscayne Bay below Miami, the area called the Hunting Grounds by the Seminoles was settled long before Columbus discovered the New World. Excavations in 1986 discovered evidence of more than 10,000 years of human habitation.

By the turn of this century, the area had become the town of Cutler with its own post office, general store, and hotel, the Richmond Inn. In 1915, Charles Deering (his brother James built Vizcaya) bought the 36-family community, dredged a new channel into the bay, and built a turning basin.

Under the guidance of architect Phineas Paist, Deering built a fireproof stone house (1922) next to his newly renovated white-columned Richmond Inn. The new residence was designed to house a large part of his extensive art collection.

Now owned by the state of Florida and operated by the Metro-Dade Park and Recreation Department, the Charles Deering Estate is the scene of the Chowder Party of the Biscayne Bay Yacht Club, held annually on George Washington's birthday.

CORAL CASTLE

Sometimes called America's Stonehenge, the
Coral Castle was built singlehandedly by 5-foot-
tall, 100-pound Lithuanian émigré Edward Leedskalnin as a shrine to his old-world fiancée, who
broke off their engagement the night before the
wedding.

Using only hand tools and working in a then-
remote area below Miami (near present-day
Homestead), Leedskalnin carved a coral rock
(oolitic limestone) palace for his beloved, with a
throne room, an observatory with stone replicas of
the moon and planets and a 20-ton "telescope," a
huge heart-shaped table, and a 20-ton gate that
can be moved with the touch of a finger.

Leedskalnin's lady love never saw her coral
castle, and the builder died a hermit, leaving un-
answered the question of how this small man was
able, unaided, to carve and handle such huge
stone monuments.

MIAMI METROZOO

About five miles west of the Charles Deering Estate, the 290-acre cageless Miami Metrozoo has
more than 2,800 wild animals in residence. The
zoo has a world-famous 1½-acre tropical aviary, a
petting zoo, more than 3 miles of walkways, and
its own air-conditioned monorail.

◄

TROPICAIRE FLEA MARKET

Drive-in motion picture theaters are pretty much a thing of the past across the country. Most are either desolate and forgotten or have been replaced by parking lots and new commercial buildings. But the old Tropicaire Drive-In on Bird Road (SW 40th Street) and the Palmetto Expressway west of Coral Gables still lives as the Tropicaire Flea Market.

►

MIAMI INTERNATIONAL AIRPORT

Only one other airport in the United States carries more international cargo and passengers than Miami International Airport. Located six miles from downtown Miami (skyscrapers in the background rise from the early morning haze), the airport has seven concourses and one hundred gates and serves eighty-three airlines.

OPA-LOCKA CITY HALL

In 1921, aviation pioneer Glen Curtiss and rancher James Bright began to subdivide their 100,000-acre ranch northwest of Miami into three communities: Hialeah, Country Club Estates (now Miami Springs), and Opa-locka, a name Curtiss simplified from the Indian *Opatishawock-alocka* (a large tree-covered island in a swamp).

Curtiss and New York architect Bernard Muller agreed upon an Arabian Nights theme for the new development. The city hall, located on Ali-Baba Avenue, was completed only a few weeks before the disastrous hurricane of 1926 marked the end of the Florida land boom of the 1920s.

The Opa-locka City Hall has recently been restored, and much of the town has been designated on the National Register of Historic Places as a "thematic resource."

HIALEAH PARK

A classical French Mediterranean setting for thoroughbred racing, Hialeah Park was built on 228 acres in 1925, planned as a centerpiece for the new city of Hialeah. Originally, the complex included a roller coaster, a jai-ali court, and a Miccosukee Indian village, but the only remainder of the optimism of 1926 is the track itself, scene of some of the most celebrated races in the country. The track is now surrounded by an industrial district. Hialeah Park, with its resident flock of 400 flamingos, is on the National Register of Historic Places.

49

◄
JOE ROBBIE STADIUM

Joe Robbie, longtime owner of the Miami Dolphins professional football team, built a new stadium about sixteen miles northwest of downtown Miami, arranged for private financing of the $100-million structure, and saw the 160-acre site open in 1987. Seating 74,919, the stadium has a playing surface of grass and extensive built-in drainage.

►
CALDER RACE COURSE

Florida's largest air-conditioned and glass-enclosed sports facility, the Calder Race Course opened in 1971 and is located less than a mile north of Joe Robbie Stadium on Florida's Turnpike.

MONASTERY OF SAINT BERNARD DE CLAIRVAUX

The oldest building in the Western Hemisphere is located in North Miami Beach. However, the cloisters of the Monastery of Saint Bernard were originally built in Segovia, Spain, from 1133 to 1141. After a revolution in the 1830s, the monastery was converted into a granary and stable. Nearly a century later, in 1926, William Randolph Hearst bought the cloisters for a half million dollars, planning to reconstruct it on his California estate, San Simeon. Workmen dismantled the ancient structure, packing the hand-carved stones in straw in eleven thousand individually numbered boxes.

Unfortunately, there was an outbreak of hoof and mouth disease in Segovia, and the U.S. Department of Agriculture quarantined the shipment when it arrived in New York. Workmen opened the wooden boxes and burned the straw packing, leaving piles of boxes and unnumbered stones—a half-million-dollar jigsaw puzzle.

The stones remained in a Brooklyn warehouse for twenty-six years. W. Edgemon and R. Moss brought them to this site in 1952 and spent another $1.5 million to reassemble the cloisters.

The Episcopal Diocese of South Florida bought the cloisters in 1964. The ancient Spanish monastery is now an Episcopal parish church.

THE JUSTICE CENTER

Designed by Arquitectonica as an anchor for a new government center complex in North Miami, the North Dade Justice Center contains offices for the clerk of courts, the state attorney, and the public defender and has a drive-in window (lower left) for paying traffic tickets. At the top of this photograph are a fire station and a police substation.

53

◄ FLORIDA INTERNATIONAL UNIVERSITY

The North Miami campus of Florida International University is located near the north end of Biscayne Bay. FIU enrolls 19,500 students, split between the University Park campus on the site of the old Tamiami Airport (it opened in 1972 with 5,800 students) and the new campus in North Miami (built in 1988).

The university has achieved national recognition for its international studies and hospitality management programs. The School of Hospitality Management is headquartered on the North Miami campus.

In this view, looking southeast, the northern end of Miami Beach lies at top left and center. The Miami skyline is visible at upper right, down Biscayne Bay.

► BARRY UNIVERSITY

In the community of Miami Shores, about seven miles due north of downtown Miami, is the 90-acre campus of Barry University, which celebrated its fiftieth anniversary in 1990. Barry College opened in 1940 with 47 students and 14 instructors (11 Sisters of Saint Dominic, 1 Dominican father, and 2 lay persons) and was the only Catholic women's college south of Washington, D.C., and east of New Orleans.

Barry began accepting male students in 1975. It became Barry University in 1982 and has a total enrollment of more than 5,000 students.

◄

BELLE MEADE ISLAND

Residences line the edge of Belle Meade Island (foreground), about five miles north of downtown Miami. In the background at upper right are the towers of the Palm Bay Club, facing Legion Park Picnic Island.

►

MARRIOTT MARINA

Facing Biscayne Bay just north of the Venetian Causeway is the Marriott Marina (center right). Behind it (to the west) is the Omni mall, an extensive shopping center just north of the skyscrapers of downtown Miami (center left). Between the Venetian and MacArthur causeways, just to the south of the Marriott complex, is the Miami *Herald* building.

FREEDOM TOWER

Designed by architects Schultze & Weaver for the Miami *Daily News* and built in 1925, the Freedom Tower was patterned after the Giralda bell tower of the cathedral in Seville, Spain. (Schultze & Weaver also incorporated the bell tower's design into their plan for the Biltmore Hotel in Coral Gables.) Floodlighted at night, the tower was registered as a federal lighthouse. It could be seen up to fifty miles at sea, according to an early Miami *Daily News* account.

In the 1960s, the tower served as the Cuban Refugee Center, processing more than half a million refugees and acquiring the name Freedom Tower. It was renovated in 1988 for use as an office building.

DOWNTOWN MIAMI

In this wide-angle photograph (looking southeast across downtown Miami), the Mitchell Wolfson campus of the Miami-Dade Community College occupies the center of the picture. The federal courthouse is in the lower center. Center left is Bayside Marketplace. Beyond it, in Biscayne Bay, are the cruise ship terminal on Dodge Island and Miami Beach (in the distance at upper left). Fisher Island, Virginia Key, and Key Biscayne from the eastern limits of Biscayne Bay. The Atlantic Ocean is in the background.

◀

CENTRAL BAPTIST CHURCH

The Central Baptist Church congregation was organized in 1896 and moved into its own building five years later. One of the organizers, John Sewell, was the construction foreman at the Royal Palm Hotel being built for Henry Flagler. Sewell was to become Miami's third mayor.

In 1927, Sewell broke the ground for a new 4-story building at 500 NE 1st Avenue. The new auditorium held 2,500 people and is still in use. Central Baptist saved the windows of its 1901 building and incorporated them into the new structure's lower level, today the social hall. An education building was added in 1950.

Just south of the church building is a Metromover station.

▶

MIAMI-DADE COMMUNITY COLLEGE

Within a curve of the Miami Metromover city public transportation system lies the Mitchell Wolfson campus of the Miami-Dade Community College (center). In this view (looking south across downtown Miami), the red-tiled federal courthouse is at right, across NE 1st Avenue from the campus.

MIAMI BOOK FAIR

Each year in November, the Mitchell Wolfson campus of Miami-Dade Community College becomes the locale of the Miami Book Fair, which attracts approximately 400,000 book lovers, publishers, authors, and booksellers. Its week-long series of events culminates in a three-day street fair where more than 300 national and international publishers display their newest books. During the fair, more than 140 well-known authors lecture, read their latest works, and autograph their books.

DADE COUNTY COURTHOUSE

A. Ten Eyck Brown and August Geiger designed the ziggurat-peaked, 360-foot-tall Dade County Courthouse (foreground, center), completed in 1928. Faced with terra cotta, the courthouse was the tallest building not only in Florida but also below Washington, D.C.

On the opposite side of the Metromover tracks from the courthouse, at 101 West Flagler Street, is the 3.3-acre Metro-Dade Cultural Center (1983). Designed by architect Philip Johnson, the red-tiled, Mediterranean-style center includes two museums and the main public library, all opening onto a plaza elevated above street level. The Center for the Fine Arts (an exhibition gallery), the Historical Museum of Southern Florida, and the library occupy separate buildings facing the tan- and brick-colored quarry-tiled plaza.

◄

BAYFRONT PARK

Downtown, between Biscayne Boulevard and the bay, is Bayfront Park, for which land was dredged starting in 1924. The park was recently redesigned by sculptor and landscape architect Isamu Noguchi. At left is the entrance to Bayside Marketplace and Miamarina; the park's amphitheater is at right. At lower center is the plaza of the Torch of Friendship.

►

SOUTHEAST FINANCIAL CENTER

The tallest building on the Miami skyline is the 55-story tower of the Southeast Financial Center, designed by Edward C. Bassett of Skidmore, Owings & Merrill of San Francisco. Connected at left is an associated 15-story annex containing parking on its upper levels and a banking lobby on the ground floor. At right are the Florida National tower and the Chopin Plaza at the south end of Bayfront Park. The parking lot at lower left becomes, on New Year's Eve, the staging area for the Orange Parade.

65

SAILING ON BISCAYNE BAY

The annual Columbus Day Regatta begins south of the Rickenbacker Causeway, which links Brickell Hammock (left), just south of the Miami River, with Virginia Key and Key Biscayne. The regatta draws more than five hundred racing yachts, which cross the starting line in a series of seventeen starts on an October Saturday morning, proceed to Elliott's Key, about eleven miles south of Miami, and anchor for the night in a huge raft of more than three thousand boats and twelve thousand competitors and well-wishers.

The following day, yachtsmen race back up the bay to Miami.

◀

STILTSVILLE

Jet skiers race past weekend houses of "Stiltsville" in Biscayne Bay below Key Biscayne. The raised camps stand on submerged leased land, spoil from the dredging of Biscayne channel. Leases will not be renewed after the turn of the century.

PART THREE

KEY BISCAYNE, BISCAYNE BAY, AND MIAMI BEACH

CAPE FLORIDA LIGHTHOUSE

At least ten years before Fort Dallas was built on the north bank of the Miami River, the 95-foot-tall Cape Florida Lighthouse (1825) was constructed at the southern tip of Key Biscayne. It is the oldest structure originally built in south Florida.

Seminole Indians attacked the brick lighthouse in 1836 and killed the lightkeeper's assistant.

Next to the lighthouse is a keeper's home, reconstructed to the period of the early 1900s. In this view, looking north, condominiums of Key Biscayne are at middle left, and Miami Beach is in the distance, at the top of the picture. The wooded area is part of the Bill Baggs Cape Florida State Recreation Area, a 406-acre park.

PRESIDENT NIXON'S HOME

A white helicopter pad built over the waters of Biscayne Bay marks the location of the Key Biscayne home used occasionally by President Richard M. Nixon. The house was totally changed and considerably enlarged by a subsequent owner. The Miami skyline is in the background.

◄

KEY COLONY CONDOMINIUM

Built in four phases in the late 1970s and early
1980s, Key Biscayne's Key Colony Condominium
luxury residential complex on Crandon Boulevard
comprises twelve hundred units on forty-one
acres in Key Biscayne. Sandy & Babcock are the
architects.

►

VIRGINIA KEY AND KEY BISCAYNE

The Rickenbacker Causeway crosses Virginia Key
(foreground) and Bear Cut (center) to become
Crandon Boulevard on Key Biscayne. In this
southeasterly view, the Atlantic Ocean is at top
left and Biscayne Bay is at right. On Virginia Key
on the far (south) side of the causeway are the
University of Miami Marine Lab and the Miami
Seaquarium.

74

◄
FISHER ISLAND

Between Virginia Key and Miami Beach is Fisher Island, created in 1905 when Government Cut (to the north of the island, not shown in this view) was dredged to make a deeper channel for the port of Miami. On the south side of the island, William Kissam Vanderbilt II built his Italianate winter residence (center) on seven acres. Vanderbilt swapped his yacht, the *Eagle*, for the land, owned by Miami Beach developer Carl Fisher.

The $1.5-million estate, with seven marble fireplaces, an immense gourmet kitchen, mahogany paneling, its own marina, private beach, and hotel-sized swimming pool, has now become the clubhouse and headquarters for a private club community: Fisher Island. Access to the island is only by boat or helicopter.

►
FLAGLER ISLAND AND MONUMENT

The winter of 1895 set records for the coldest temperatures since Americans had been keeping track, and in Palm Beach, where Henry Flagler had terminated the southward progress of his Florida East Coast Railroad, orange trees were freezing.

Julia Tuttle, the widow of a Cleveland, Ohio, industrialist, owned six hundred acres on the northern bank of the mouth of the Miami River where it meets Biscayne Bay. She offered Flagler half of her property for a townsite if he would bring his railroad that far south.

Following the freeze, Flagler sent his land agent, J. E. Ingraham, to investigate the Miami climate, and he returned with green foliage and blossoming flowers from Mrs. Tuttle's property.

Flagler brought his railroad to Miami and built the Royal Palm Hotel on former Tuttle holdings. Later, Miami built a monument to his memory on Flagler Island in Biscayne Bay. Julia Tuttle is memorialized only by a causeway.

STAR ISLAND

Entered by a single, guarded gateway, Star Island is one of three residential islands (Palm, Hibiscus, and Star) off the MacArthur Causeway, which connects downtown Miami with the south point of Miami Beach.

Celebrated residents of these islands have included Don Johnson of the television series *Miami Vice*; Damon Runyan, author; and Al Capone, Chicago racketeer.

VENETIAN ISLANDS

Collins Bridge, a 2½-mile-long wooden structure, was the first bridge to connect Miami Beach (then variously named Alton Beach, Ocean Beach, or Miami Beach) with Miami. The bridge was replaced by the Venetian Causeway in 1925. Artificial islands along the causeway include Rivo Alto (foreground), Dilido, San Marino, San Marco, and Biscayne Island (closest to Miami). At upper left are Hibiscus and Palm islands and the MacArthur Causeway.

◄ BISCAYNE ISLAND

The last of the islands along the Venetian Causeway to be filled in was Biscayne Island, foreground, an airstrip in the early 1930s. Toward the
east in this view are the islands along the Venetian
Causeway and Miami Beach. At right center are
part of Watson Island and the MacArthur Causeway. Hibiscus, Palm, and Star islands are at center
right, and Dodge, Lummus, and Fisher islands
are in the distance, along Government Cut.

► MIAMI BEACH'S SOUTH POINTE

At the southern tip of Miami Beach are, at left,
South Pointe Park and South Pointe Tower, the
tall building overlooking Government Cut, which
separates South Pointe from Fisher Island (upper
left). Across Biscayne Street (center) from South
Pointe Tower is Penrod's Beach Club, the red-
roofed building on the beach. The South Pointe
section of Miami Beach is a favorite area for wind
surfing and jet skiing. Downtown Miami is in the
background, to the west.

◄

OLD MIAMI BEACH

An aerial photograph taken February 25, 1930, indicates that Miami Beach had recovered from the hurricane of 1926, but the area, now sometimes called "Old Miami Beach," had yet to experience its Art Deco boom, which occurred during the late 1930s and the early 1940s.

Ocean Drive, with a park between it and the beach, is at upper right. Parallel to it, from right, are Collins Avenue, Washington Avenue, Pennsylvania Avenue, and Euclid Avenue, at left. The tall building in the center, between Washington and Pennsylvania avenues in the 800 block, is the Blackstone, built by Kingston Hall in 1929. Near the top of the picture is the nine-story city hall, designed by architect Martin Luther Hampton in 1927. Between the Blackstone and the city hall, on the opposite side of the street, is the Washington Storage Company.

Photo courtesy Historical Association of Southern Florida

▶

MIAMI BEACH TODAY

At right and on overleaf are contemporary views of Miami Beach and the Art Deco district, a square mile of which became the nation's first twentieth-century district placed on the National Register of Historic Places.

◄
OCEAN DRIVE

Miami Beach's Ocean Drive has recently under-
gone a $2.4-million refurbishing, complementing
the grand old Art Deco hotels that overlook the
beach. In this view of the 1200, 1300, and 1400
blocks of Ocean Drive, looking northwest, Lummus Park is in the foreground. At extreme left
on Ocean Drive are the Ocean Front apartments,
the Leslie Hotel (1927), and the Carlyle (1941).
Across 13th Street are the Cardozo (1939) and adjacent Cavalier (1936) hotels.

   In addition to the funds spent by the city, $20
million has been contributed by private investors
for the restoration, renovation, and adaptation of
the Art Deco hotels in the ten-block section of
Ocean Drive between 5th and 15th streets.

▶
COLLINS AVENUE HOTELS

In the 1940s and early 1950s, taller hotels were
built on Collins Avenue north of Ocean Drive
(which stops at 15th Street). In the 1800 block of
Collins are the Shore Club hotel, the Nautilus,
and the Shelborne (1954), designed by Igor B.
Polevitsky.

   Hotels in the 1700 and 1600 blocks of Collins
Avenue (overleaf) include, left to right, the Raleigh
(1940), designed by L. Murray Dixon, the Richmond, the South Seas (1941), the Marseilles, the
Hotel Del Caribe (1948), designed by MacKay &
Gibbs, the Surfcomber, the Ritz Plaza, the Delano
(1947), the National (1940), and the Sagamore.

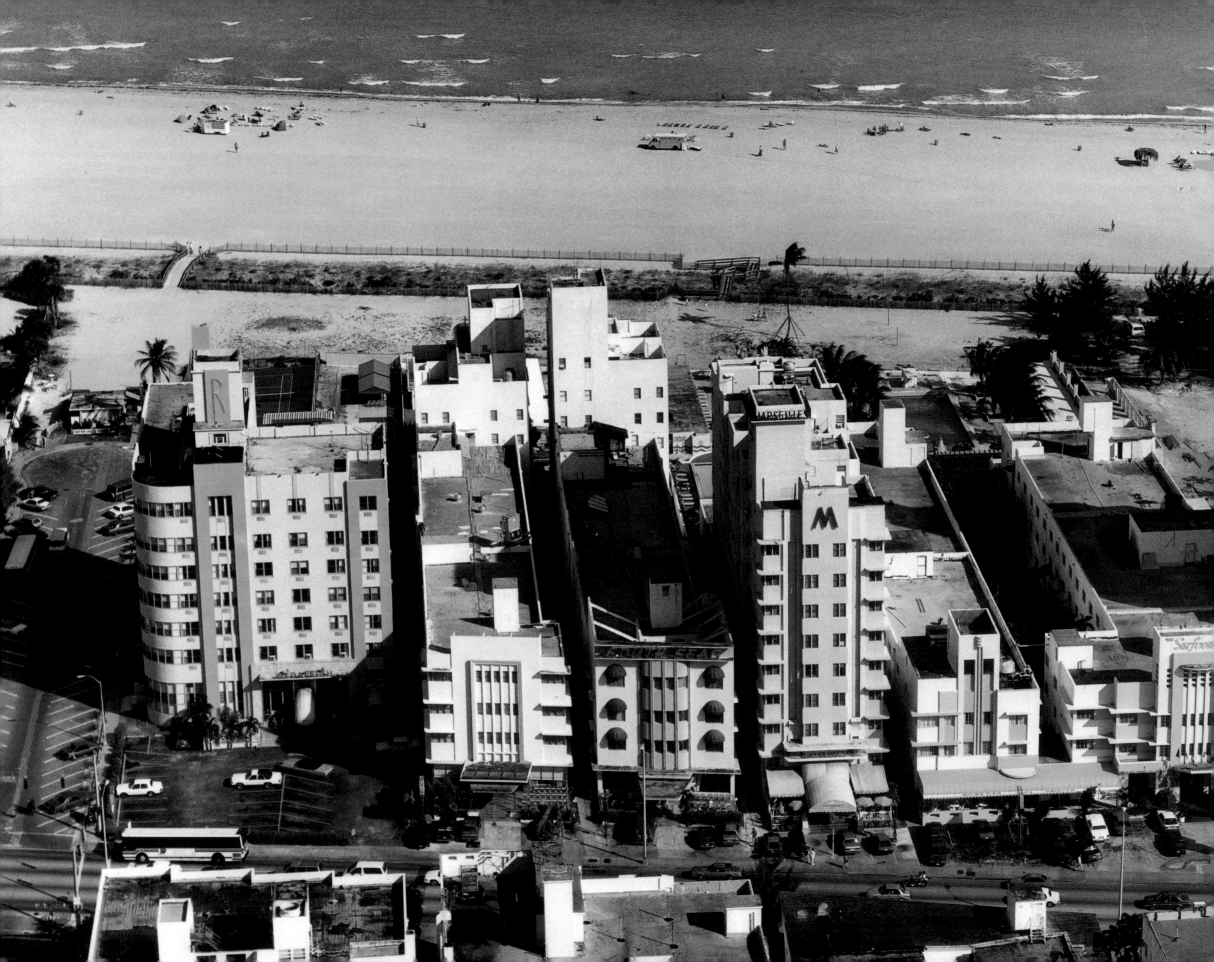

WASHINGTON STORAGE COMPANY

When the wealthy winter residents of Miami Beach in the late 1920s and 1930s returned to the North in the spring, they stored their valuable furniture, drapes, carpeting—and sometimes their automobiles—for six to nine months of the year in the dehumidified quarters of the Washington Storage Company, designed by Robertson & Patterson.

The Matthews family built the three-story Spanish Mediterranean warehouse in 1927 and added two more floors in 1932. The family continued to own and operate Washington Storage until it was bought by Mitchell Wolfson, Jr., in 1985. Wolfson added two more floors in 1989 and is converting the storage facility into a museum to house the Mitchell Wolfson, Jr., Collection of Decorative and Propaganda Arts.

SUNSET ISLANDS

Hotels in the vicinity of 17th Street and Collins Avenue are in the background as one looks southwest across Miami Beach's Sunset Islands. Seventeen islands are included within the city limits of Miami Beach.

◄

THE FOUNTAINEBLEAU

At a sudden bend in the road, where northbound Collins Avenue joins Indian Creek Drive, one's first view of the Fountainebleau Hilton Hotel and Spa is through a giant arch—a 13,000-square-foot *trompe l'oeil* mural by Richard Haas. The mural, which frames a painted Fountainebleau through a painted arch, was dedicated in 1986. The Fountainebleau was opened in 1954, the largest hotel in Florida: 1,250 rooms, with a convention hall that has been the site of three presidential conventions.

The Fountainebleau was one of architect Morris Lapidus' first great commissions. He later fashioned more than 200 hotels worldwide.

►

THE EDEN ROC

Just north of the Fountainebleau is another Morris Lapidus creation, the Eden Roc hotel (right). Completed in the mid-1950s, it stands adjacent to the windowless north elevation of the Fountainebleau's seventeen-story North Tower. Not a Lapidus design, the tower was completed about the same time as the Eden Roc.

◀

LA GORCE COUNTRY CLUB

About three miles north of the Art Deco district is the golf course of the La Gorce Country Club, a development that Carl Fisher named for a close friend, Oliver La Gorce, president of the National Geographic Society.

▶

ISLANDS IN BISCAYNE BAY

At the northern limits of Miami Beach, Stillwater Drive is in the foreground as one looks south on Biscayne Bay. Beyond Cleveland and Daytona roads (center) lies Normandy Shores Golf Course. Beyond Normandy Shores are La Gorce Island and its golf course, upper left, and part of Treasure Island (in Miami, not Miami Beach), upper right. In the distance, a typical summer morning thundershower marches across Biscayne Bay.

◀

INDIAN CREEK

Just north of the city limits of Miami Beach is Indian Creek, an island enclave of the rich and/or famous. Julio Iglesias is a landowner here. The Miami skyline is in the distance to the south.

▶

BAL HARBOUR AND HAULOVER CUT

North of Miami Beach are the villages of Bal Harbour (its northern limits end at Haulover Cut, right) and, farther to the south, Surfside. The two towns face the Atlantic Ocean and its broad, sandy, man-made beach, which ends ten miles to the south at Government Cut. Indian Creek forms their western boundary.

Erosion had seriously threatened the beach and its adjacent hotels by the mid-1970s, but the U.S. Army Corps of Engineers began a four-year project in 1977 to rebuild the strand, visited annually by about ten million people, to a width of three hundred feet.

AVENTURA CONDOMINIUMS

The Aventura condominiums and the golf course of the Biscayne Bay Yacht and Country Club are located in Dade County's northeast corner, to the north of the William Lehman Causeway (upper right corner).

PART FOUR

BROWARD AND PALM BEACH COUNTIES

◄

FORT LAUDERDALE

A containerized freight ship leaves Port Everglades at Fort Lauderdale, the county seat of
Broward County. The business district is to the
northwest in the upper third of this view. Overlooking the channel is the Fort Lauderdale Marriott Hotel and Marina. The Intracoastal Waterway parallels the beach.

►

THE VENICE OF AMERICA

Called the Venice of America, Fort Lauderdale,
with 165 miles of navigable waterways, has more
miles of canals than does that famous Italian city.
In this view, the Atlantic Ocean, to the east, fills
the top of the picture. The Intracoastal Waterway
parallels the beach. In the foreground is the Rio
Vista development.

PIER 66

The Pier 66 Hotel and Marina was built on the Intracoastal Waterway by Phillips Petroleum as Fort Lauderdale's first luxury high-rise resort hotel. A revolving cocktail lounge at the top turns, predictably, at 66 revolutions per minute. SE 17th Street (left) heads west across a drawbridge on the Intracoastal Waterway as brightly lit pleasure craft prepare for the annual Winterfest Boat Parade.

▶ WINTERFEST BOAT PARADE

Held the second weekend in December, Fort Lauderdale's annual Winterfest Boat Parade draws half a million spectators who come to see gaily decorated and illuminated boats glide along the Intracoastal Waterway.

◄

SIX FLAGS ATLANTIS

In Hollywood, Florida, lies one of the largest water parks in the country: Six Flags Atlantis. The park has forty-five pools, seven-story water slides, wave pools (top center), a maze (center left), and an activity pool (foreground). This view shows only a relatively small part of the park, located just off I-95 (upper left) in the southern part of Broward County.

▶

ALONG THE HILLSBORO MILE

A "cigarette boat," so named for its long, sleek shape, speeds north on the Intracoastal Waterway along the Hillsboro Mile, a section of beach between Fort Lauderdale and Boca Raton.

103

STRANAHAN HOUSE

Frank Stranahan came to Fort Lauderdale in 1892 and established trade with the Indians. His original store and home still overlook New River in downtown Fort Lauderdale. The Stranahan House, now a museum, contains a number of original Stranahan furnishings.

104

NEW RIVER AND DOWNTOWN FORT LAUDERDALE

In 1796, the Spanish granted land on the New River in their territory of Florida to one Franke Lewis, but there were no permanent white settlers until after 1835, when a man named Colee cleared land and planted coconuts at an old Indian campsite. Colee's wife and family were killed during an uprising. Major William Lauderdale established a fort at the river's mouth in 1838. The New River still flows from the now-cultivated Everglades (top of picture). In the background at center are the towers of present-day Fort Lauderdale.

HILLSBORO LIGHTHOUSE

Located where the Hillsboro Inlet connects the Intracoastal Waterway with the Atlantic Ocean, the Hillsboro Lighthouse, one of the most powerful in the country, has provided a beacon for sailors since 1907.

Hotels of Pompano Beach line the seashore to the south, toward the top of this photograph. Fort Lauderdale is on the horizon.

BOCA RATON HOTEL AND CLUB

At the Boca Raton Inlet, which provides access from the Atlantic Ocean to the Intracoastal Waterway and Boca Raton Lake, is the Boca Raton Hotel and Club. The original building, the Cloister Inn, across Boca Raton Lake, was built by architect Addison Mizner in 1926. In 1961, the tower was added, and in 1981, the Boca Beach Club was built on the Boca Inlet.

◄

PALM BEACH RESIDENCES

Palm Beach's residences are famous for their immaculately trimmed hedges. This view shows the north end of Tarpon Island on Lake Worth.

►

MAR-A-LAGO

Called "Florida's most sybaritic private residence" by Hap Hatton, author of *An Architectural History of Florida*, Mar-A-Lago was cereal heiress Marjorie Merriweather Post's 118-room Palm Beach winter home.

Completed in January, 1927, the pink fantasy mansion was built on 17.7 acres that extend from the Atlantic to Lake Worth. The estate required a staff of 80 during peak periods and contains 58 bedrooms, 32 bathrooms, and 27 servants' rooms. Mar-A-Lago was designed by architect Marion Sims Wyeth and set designer Joseph Urban, and each of the major rooms has its own architectural-historical style: the master bedroom after Versailles, a Williamsburg formal bedroom, a Sleeping Beauty suite, a fifteenth-century Italian dining room, and a living room more like the grandest of motion picture palaces of the late 1920s.

Mrs. Post willed the great house to the U.S. government in 1973, but it was returned to the Post Foundation in 1980. Now owned by Donald J. Trump, Mar-A-Lago is once again a Palm Beach winter residence.

THE BREAKERS

Henry Flagler, the famous railroad magnate who made Palm Beach an internationally acclaimed resort, built the Palm Beach Inn on this site in 1895. It burned in 1903, but Flagler immediately replaced it with a larger, finer structure, renamed The Breakers.

A second fire in 1925 razed the hotel, but the Flagler heirs retained Leonard Schultze, architect of the Waldorf-Astoria in New York, to design an Italian Renaissance palace worthy of the memory of Henry Flagler, who had died twelve years earlier.

For 11½ months, 1,200 craftsmen worked shifts around the clock to complete the new Breakers by December 26, 1926. It was quickly called the finest resort hotel in America.

The Flagler System, continuing the original ownership, expanded The Breakers in 1969, adding two oceanfront wings.

Guests of The Breakers have included John D. Rockefeller, J. P. Morgan, and Andrew Carnegie, as well as every U.S. president since Warren G. Harding.

WHITEHALL

In 1901, near the site of The Breakers, Henry Flagler built a 55-room cottage for his third wife, Mary Lily Kenan, retaining architects Carrere and Hastings, who had designed hotels for him in Saint Augustine. The $2.5-million mansion was completed in eighteen months. Another $1.5 million was spent for furnishings, which included the world's largest pipe organ. The 40- by 110-foot entrance foyer, "Marble Hall," has an elaborate frescoed ceiling and is finished in 7 varieties of marble.

In 1926, the family opened the mansion as the Whitehall Hotel, with an added 300-room, 11-story tower on the western side. The tower was demolished by Flagler's granddaughter Jean Flagler Matthews when she opened Whitehall as a house museum in 1960 with many of its original furnishings.

WEST PALM BEACH

Henry Flagler founded West Palm Beach, on the western side of Lake Worth, as a community primarily for the workers, craftsmen, and servants of the great estates of Palm Beach. Today it is the commercial center and county seat of Palm Beach County.

Lake Worth, in this view, extends northward, and condominiums face the waterfront. The approach to the Royal Palm Bridge is at right center, and the Flagler Memorial Bridge is at upper right.

LAKE OKEECHOBEE

Orange groves and sugarcane fields line the shores of Lake Okeechobee, the southern tip of which is about forty-five miles west of Palm Beach. The lake is the major source of fresh water for much of south Florida, including Miami, Fort Lauderdale, and West Palm Beach.

◀
THE EVERGLADES

A "river of grass," the Everglades once extended continuously from Lake Okeechobee to Florida Bay, more than a hundred miles south. Now much of the northern part of the Glades has been "reclaimed"—drained and cleared—for agriculture, and burgeoning subdivisions crowd the shoreline from Palm Beach to Miami.

Parts of the Everglades contain Seminole and Miccosukee Indian reservations. Airboat tours of the Everglades have become an economic mainstay for the tribes.

▶
MICCOSUKEE VILLAGE

A Miccosukee-owned airboat approaches an Indian settlement in the Everglades to the west of Miami.

◀

EVERGLADES NATIONAL PARK

Below the northern edge of the Everglades National Park, created in 1947, stands the Shark Valley Observation Tower, built on the site of a 1940s oil well. Butane-powered trams carry visitors from the park entrance on the Tamiami Trail (U.S. 41) seven miles south to the tower.

▶

JOHN PENNECAMP CORAL REEF STATE PARK

One of the favorite haunts for skin divers in south Florida is the John Pennecamp Coral Reef State Park (established in 1960) off Key Largo. America's first undersea park, the park reservation covers the northern end of the coral reef that parallels the Florida Keys from Key Largo to the Dry Tortugas. The taking of coral is now against the law in the Keys, but underwater sightseers are welcome to explore the 75-square-mile park with its 400 species of fish and dozens of varieties of living coral.

◄
ALLIGATOR REEF LIGHTHOUSE

Alligator Lighthouse, considered the most beautiful on the reef and one of the finest iron lighthouses in the world, was built in 1873 and stands on Alligator Reef, off the Matecumbe Keys, about twenty-five miles southwest of Key Largo.

It is one of six iron-pile structures built between 1852 and 1880 on the Florida Reef between Key Biscayne and Key West. The reef seemed almost a magnet for ships. Before the lights were erected, vessels going aground averaged about one a week, supporting a thriving salvage industry headquartered in Key West.

►
MARATHON AND KEY VACA

The community of Marathon on Key Vaca, about halfway down the keys, began as a railroad town during the construction, in the early 1900s, of Henry Flagler's Overseas Railroad, which continued his Florida East Coast Railroad from Miami to Key West. By 1906, the epic road had made it as far as Key Vaca, but it took another five years to build the Seven-Mile Bridge connecting Key Vaca with the keys to the west.

The four-story wooden lighthouse in the center foreground is the 1940s Faro Blanco Lighthouse, part of the Faro Blanco Resort and Marina extending from the water in the foreground to the Overseas Highway (U.S. 1) across the center of this photograph.

◀
BAHIA HONDA BRIDGE

The most difficult construction on the Overseas Railroad was the 6,734-foot Bahia Honda (Deep Water) Bridge, shorter than the Seven-Mile Bridge but spanning much deeper water. It also required a higher, cantilevered design. When the Overseas Highway for automobiles replaced the hurricane-damaged railroad in 1936, engineers utilized the rail line's bridges, building a widened roadway over the old piers.

At the Bahia Honda Bridge, however, the design of the bridge prevented a widened roadbed at rail level, so a separate roadway was built across the top of the old bridge (in this view, to the left of the new four-lane automobile bridge completed only a few years ago).

▶
KEY WEST

Key West, named *Cayo Hueso* (Island of Bones) by the Spanish in the 1500s, was a port favored by pirates until Commodore David Porter ran them out in 1830 with his West India Squadron.

Salvagers of ships wrecked on the Florida Reef made a handsome living in Key West until the reef lighthouses erected between 1852 and 1880 brought an end to the era of profitable wrecking. By the 1880s, cigar factories and sponge fishing boosted the island economy, but growth ended about the turn of the present century.

Writers, including Ernest Hemingway and Tennessee Williams, began to come to the sleepy town in the 1930s, but the economy showed little life until after World War II. Today, Key West has become a tourist Mecca, attracting more than a million visitors annually.

HEMINGWAY HOUSE AND LIGHTHOUSE MUSEUM

Ernest Hemingway came to Key West in 1931 and bought a limestone mansion built by Asa Tift in 1851. Most Key West lots are small (30- by 50-foot lots are considered adequate), but the Tift mansion occupies a wooded acre and a half on Whitehead Street, across from an 1847 lighthouse (now a museum).

It was in Key West that Hemingway wrote *A Farewell to Arms*, *Death in the Afternoon*, *To Have and Have Not*, and *For Whom the Bell Tolls*.

MALLORY SQUARE

Mallory Square has been a favorite location for Key West visitors to watch the tropical sun go down. Cruise ships may berth at Mallory Square, but they must be gone before sunset.

◄ LOGGERHEAD KEY

A few miles to the west of Fort Jefferson is Loggerhead Key, another of the Dry Tortugas islands.
A brick lighthouse was erected there from 1856
to 1868 and has remained in continuous service. It was modernized in 1920 and is now semi-
automated. Coast Guard or Coast Guard Auxiliary
personnel maintain equipment and reside on the
lonely island. The lighthouse has been nominated
for the National Register of Historic Places.

Loggerhead Key is included in the 64,000 acres
of land and water that are part of the Fort Jefferson National Monument, administered by the National Park Service.

Fort Jefferson and the surrounding 75 square
miles, covering both land and water, were designated a national monument in 1935. More than
three hundred years earlier, in 1513, Juan Ponce
de Leon named these islands *tortugas* (tortoises)
after the great number of sea turtles in the area.
Most of the Dry Tortugas are closed during turtle
season—March through September.

► FORT JEFFERSON

The Dry Tortugas, islands seventy miles to the
west of Key West, gained their name because they
lack fresh water. Nevertheless, their location en-
couraged President Thomas Jefferson to propose
the construction of a fort on Garden Key in the
Dry Tortugas.

With eight-foot-thick brick walls that stand
fifty feet high, the fort, begun in 1846, required
nearly sixteen million bricks and ten years for
completion. The invention of the rifled cannon
rendered the fort obsolete, and during the Civil
War no shots were fired from it in anger. Used as
a prison during and following the war, its most no-
table occupant was Samuel Mudd, the physician
who set John Wilkes Booth's broken leg after Booth
assassinated Abraham Lincoln.

PART FIVE

FESTIVE MIAMI

◀

GRAND PRIX OF MIAMI

Along a 1.87-mile bayfront street circuit that includes Biscayne Boulevard and Bicentennial Park,
GTP (Grand Touring Prototype) sports cars attain
speeds up to 160 mph in the Nissan Grand Prix of
Miami. The field includes world-class drivers and
vehicles from Europe, Canada, Mexico, and Japan. Sanctioned by the International Motorsports
Association, the race is held annually in late February or early March and attracts more than
80,000 specatators.

▶

CALLE OCHO FESTIVAL

A million revelers crowd along a 23-block stretch
of SW 8th Street—Calle Ocho—during the Calle
Ocho Festival. Held each year in mid-March, the
event celebrates the heritage of Cuba and features
music, dancing, folkloric troupes from Latin
America, a variety of foods, and special attractions
for children.

CENTRUST TOWER

The CenTrust Tower's nightly illumination changes with the seasons. "Snowflakes" accent the tower during Christmastime (left). Orange lights flood CenTrust on New Year's Eve, in honor of the Orange Bowl and associated events of the Orange Festival. The area near the large Christmas tree is ablaze as participants in the King Orange Jamboree Parade start to roll.

ORANGE BOWL, 1990

Notre Dame and Colorado fans pack the Orange Bowl stadium, a well of light as darkness blankets the city on New Year's Day. The Irish won the 1990 contest.

Bayside Marketplace and the Freedom Tower

INDEX

Agam, Yacov, 14
Alligator Reef Lighthouse, 118
Alton Beach, 76
Armour, Charles W., 20
Arquitectoncia International Corporation, viii, 14, 32, 53
Art Deco: 80; hotels, 84
Art Deco district: viii, 80; mentioned, 93
Atlantis, viii, 14
Aventura condominiums, 96

Bahia Honda Bridge, 120
Bal Harbour, 94
Barnacle, 23
Barry University, 54
Bassett, Charles E., viii
Bassett, Edward C., 65
Bay of Pigs invasion, 29
Bayfront Park, viii, 2, 65
Bayside Marketplace, 58, 65, 133
Bear Cut, 73
Belle Mead Island, 56
Benjamin Thompson & Associates, viii
Bill Baggs Cape Florida State Recreation Area, 71
Biltmore Hotel, viii, 36, 58
Biltmore Hotel and County Club, 40
Bindley, John, 25
Biscayne Bay: 67, 93; mentioned, 6, 13, 14, 16, 20, 23, 26, 42, 54, 56, 58, 68, 73, 75
Biscayne Bay Yacht and Country Club, 96
Biscayne Bay Yacht Club, 20, 23, 42
Biscayne Boulevard: 2; mentioned, 65
Biscayne Island: 4, 79; mentioned, 6
Blackstone hotel, 80
Boats, cargo, 11
Boca Raton Hotel and Club, 106
Boca Raton Inlet, 106
Booth, John Wilkes, 125
Breakers, The, 36, 110, 111
Brickell Avenue: viii, 11, 13; bridge, 6, 9; condominiums, 13, 14
Brickell Hammock, 26, 67

Brigade 2506 Memorial, 29
Bright, James, 48
Brown, A. Ten Eyck, 63
Bryan Memorial Church, 25
Bryan, William Jennings, 25, 30

Calder, Alexander, 18
Calder Race Course, 50
Calle Ocho (SW 8th Street), viii, 26, 29
Calle Ocho Festival, 26, 129
Cape Florida Lighthouse, 71
Capone, Al, 76
Cardozo hotel, 84
Carlyle hotel, 84
Carnegie, Andrew, 20, 110
Carrere and Hastings, 111
Carrollton School for Girls, 25
Castro, Fidel, viii, 26
Cavalier hotel, 84
Center for the Fine Arts, 63
Central Baptist Church, 60
CenTrust Tower, viii, 6, 130
Chalfin, Paul, 16, 32
Charles Deering Estate, 42, 44
Chinese Village, Coral Gables, 38
Chopin Plaza, 65
City halls: Coral Gables, 35; Miami, 23; Miami Beach, 80; Opa-locka, 48
Cloister Inn, 106
Coconut Grove: 25; mentioned, 13, 18, 20, 23
Coconut Grove Playhouse, 20, 25
Cole, Clifford, 20
Collins, John, 4
Collins Avenue: 80, 84; mentioned, 88
Collins Bridge, 4, 76
Colonnade Building, 32
Columbus Day Regatta, 67
Coral Castle, 44
Coral Gables: viii, 30; city hall, 35; water tower, 35; waterway, 38; mentioned, 32, 36, 38, 40, 42, 46, 58
Coral Reef Yacht Club, 20

Coral rock (oolite), 20, 35, 44
Country Club Estates, 48
Country Club Prado Entrance, Coral Gables, 30
Cuban Refugee Center, 58
Curtiss, Glen, 48
Cutler, 42

Dade County Courthouse, 4, 63
De Garmo, Walter, 20, 30, 32
De Leon, Juan Ponce, 125
Deering, Charles, 42, 44
Deering, James, vii, 16, 42
Delano hotel, 84
Dinner Key Marina, 23
Dixon, L. Murray, 84
Doctor's Hospital, 40
Dodge Island: 6, 58, 79; mentioned, 9
Douglas Entrance, Coral Gables, 30
Dry Tortugas: 125; mentioned, 117
Dutch South African Village, 38

Eden Roc hotel, viii, 90
Edgemon, W., 53
El Jardin, 25
Elliott's Key, 67
Engle, George, 20
Episcopal Diocese of South Florida, 53
Ermita de la Caridad, 18
Everglades: 105, 115; Club, vii; National Park, 117

Faro Blanco: Lighthouse, 118; Resort and Marina, 118
Federal courthouse, 58, 60
Federal Express/Orange Bowl Football Classic, 13
Field, Marshall, 20
Fink, Denman, 30, 35
Fisher, Carl, viii, 75, 93
Fisher Island:, 75, 79; mentioned, 58
Flagler, Henry Morrison: vii, 9, 25, 75, 110, 111, 113, 118; mentioned, 60
Flagler Island and Monument, 75
Flagler System, 110

Flagler Workers House, 6, 9
Florida East Coast Railroad: 25, 118; mentioned, 75
Florida International University, 54
Florida National tower, 65
Fort Dallas: 6, 71; Park, 9
Fort Jefferson National Monument, 125
Fort Lauderdale: viii, 99, 104, 105; mentioned, 103, 106, 113
Fort Lauderdale Marriott Hotel and Marina, 99
Fountainebleau, viii, 90
Freedom Tower, viii, 58, 133

Garden Key, 125
Giralda bell tower, viii, 36, 58
Government Cut: 79; mentioned, 26, 75, 94
Gran Prix of Miami, 2, 129
Great Depression, 38
Grove Isle, 18

Haas, Richard, 90
Hall, Kingston, 80
Hampton, Martin Luther, 80
Harding, Warren G., 110
Hatton, Hap, 108
Haulover Cut, 94
Hearst, William Randolph, 53
Hemingway, Ernest, 20, 120, 122
Hemingway House, 122
Hialeah, 48, 49
Hialeah Park, 49
Hibiscus Island, 76, 79
Hillsboro Lighthouse, 106
Hillsboro Mile, 103
Historical Museum of Southern Florida, 63
Hoffman, F. Burrall, Jr., 16
Hotel Del Caribe, 84
Hurricane of 1926, pp. 35, 38, 48, 80
Hyatt Regency Hotel, 6

I. M. Pei & Partners, viii, 6
Iglesias, Julio, 94

Imperial, viii, 14
Indian Creek, 94
Ingraham, J. E., 75
Intercap Investments, 32
Intracoastal Waterway, 99, 101, 103, 106

James L. Knight International Center, 6
Jefferson, Thomas, 125
Joe Robbie Stadium, 50
John Pennecamp Coral Reef State Park, 117
Johnson, Don, 76
Johnson, Philip, 63
José Martí Park, 10

Kenan, Mary Lily, 111
Key Biscayne: 71, 73; mentioned, 14, 58, 67, 68, 118
Key Colony Condominium, 73
Key Vaca, 118
Key West: 120, 122; mentioned, 118
King Orange Jamboree Parade, 13, 65, 130
Kooning, Willem de, 18
Krebs, Rockne, 9

La Gorce, Oliver, 93
La Gorce Country Club, 93
Lake Okeechobee, 113, 115
Lake Worth: 113; mentioned, 108
Lapidus, Morris, viii, 90
Lauderdale, William, 105
Leedskalnin, Edward, 44
Legion Park Picnic Island, 56
Leslie Hotel, 84
Lewis, Franke, 105
Lighthouse Museum, 122
Lincoln, Abraham, 125
Little Havana, viii, 26
Loggerhead Key, 125
Lummus Island: 6, 79; mentioned, 9

MacArthur Causeway: 76; mentioned, 56, 79
MacKay & Gibbs, 84
Mallory Square, 122
Mar-A-Lago, 108
Marathon, 118
Margulies, Martin C., 18
Marine Lab, University of Miami, 73
Marriott Marina, 56
Marseilles hotel, 84
Martí, José, 10, 29
Matthews, Jean Flagler, 111
Matthews family, 88
Mediterranean Revival architecture, vii, 25
Memorial Boulevard, 29
Merrick, George, viii, 30, 32, 35, 38, 40
Metro-Dade: Park and Recreation Department, 16, 42; Cultural Center, 63; Library, 63
Metromover, 60, 63
Metrorail bridge, 9
Metrozoo, 44
Miamarina, 65
Miami: downtown, 13, 58; city hall, 23; mentioned, 20, 25, 32, 46, 48, 50, 56, 76

Miami Beach: viii, 4, 76, 80; city hall, 80; mentioned, 6, 9, 54, 58, 71, 75, 76
Miami Book Fair, 62
Miami *Daily News*, 58
Miami *Herald* building, 56
Miami International Airport, 46
Miami *News* Tower, viii, 2, 36
Miami River: 2, 6, 9, 10, 11; mentioned, 13, 25, 67, 71, 75
Miami Seaquarium, 73
Miami Springs, 48
Miami-Dade Community College: 60; Mitchell Wolfson campus, 58, 60, 62
Miccosukee Indians, 115
Miracle Center, viii, 32
Miracle Mile, 32, 35
Mitchell Wolfson campus, Miami-Dade Community College, 58, 60, 62
Mitchell Wolfson, Jr., Collection of Decorative and Propaganda Arts, 88
Mizner, Addison, vii, 106
Monastery of Saint Bernard de Clairvaux, 53
Monty Trainer's Bayshore Restaurant, 20
Morgan, J. P., 110
Moss, R., 53
Mudd, Samuel, 125
Munroe, Ralph Middleton, 23

National hotel, 84
Nautilus hotel, 84
New River, 104, 105
Nixon, Richard M.: home of, 71
Noguchi, Isamu, viii, 18, 65
Norman Whitten University Center, 40
Normandy Shores, 93
North Dade: Courthouse, viii; Justice Center, 53
North Miami Beach, 53

Ocean Beach, 4, 76
Ocean Drive, 80, 84
Ocean Front apartments, 84
Old Miami Beach, 80
Omni mall, 56
Oolite (coral rock), 20, 35, 44
Opa-locka: 48; city hall, 48
Orange Bowl Festival, 13
Orange Bowl Parade. *See* King Orange Jamboree Parade
Orange Bowl stadium, 13, 132
Otto G. Richter Library, 40
Our Lady of Charity shrine, 18
Overseas Highway, 118
Overseas Railroad, 118, 120

Paist, Phineas, 30, 32, 35, 42
Palace, viii, 14
Palm Bay Club, 56
Palm Beach: 108, 110, 111; mentioned, 36, 75, 113
Palm Beach Inn, 110
Palm Island, 76, 79
Pan American Airways, 23
Parrot Jungle, 42
Penrod's Beach Club, 79

Phillips Petroleum, 101
Pier 66 Hotel and Marina, 101
Plaza de la Cubanidad, 29
Plymouth Congregational Church, 25
Polevitsky, Igor B., 84
Pompano Beach, 106
Porter, David, 120
Post Foundation, 108
Post, Marjorie Merriweather, 108
Prado Entrance, Coral Gables, 30

Raleigh hotel, 84
Richmond hotel, 84
Richmond Inn, 42
Richter, Otto G., 40
Rickenbacker Causeway, 67, 73
Rio Vista development, 99
Ritz Plaza hotel, 84
Robbie, Joe, 50
Robertson & Patterson, 88
Rockefeller, John D., 110
Royal Palm Cottages, 9
Royal Palm Hotel: 2, 9, 75; mentioned, 60
Runyan, Damon, 76

Sagamore hotel, 84
Sandy & Babcock, 73
School of Hospitality Management, 54
Schultze, Leonard, 110
Schultze & Weaver, viii, 36, 58
Seminole Indians, 42, 71, 115
Seven-Mile Bridge, 118, 120
Sewell, John, 60
Shark Valley Observation Tower, 117
Shelborne hotel, 84
Shenandoah, 26
Shore Club hotel, 84
Silver Bluff, 20
Singer, Paris, vii
Sisters of Saint Dominic, 54
Six Flags Atlantis, 103
Skidmore, Owings & Merrill, viii, 65
Society of the Sacred Heart, 25
South Pointe Park, 79
South Pointe Tower, 79
South Seas hotel, 84
Southeast Financial Center, viii, 6, 65
Star Island, 76, 79
Stillwater Drive, 93
Stiltsville, 68
Stranahan, Frank, 104
Stranahan House, 104
Suarez, Diego, 16
Sunset Islands, 88
Surfcomber hotel, 84
Surfside, 94
SW 8th Street, 26

Tamiami Trail: 26, 30; mentioned, 117
Tarpon Island, 108
Tift, Asa, 122
Torch of Friendship, 65

Tropicaire Flea Market, 46
Trump, Donald J., 108
Tuttle, Julia, vii, 75

U.S. Army Corps of Engineers, 94
University of Miami: 13, 40; Marine Lab, 73
Urban, Joseph, 108

Vanderbilt, William Kissam II, 75
Venetian Causeway: 4, 76, 79; mentioned, 56
Venetian Islands, 76
Venetian Pool, 30
Villa Regina, 14
Villa Rezzonico, 16
Virginia Key: 73; mentioned, 58, 67, 75
Vizcaya Museum and Gardens: vii, 16, 32, 42; mentioned, 18

Waldorf-Astoria hotel, 36, 110
Washington Storage Company, 80, 88
Water tower, Coral Gables, 35
Watson Island: 4; mentioned, 6, 79
Weismuller, Johnny, 30
West India Squadron, 120
West Palm Beach, 113
Whitehall, vii, 111
William Dorsky & Associates, 14
Williams, Esther, 30
Williams, Tennessee, 120
Winterfest Boat Parade, 101
Wolfson, Mitchell, Jr., 88
Wyeth, Marion Sims, 38, 108